LOTHAR TRAMPERT

SEE YOU © ARTIST IMAGES

AF222369

SEE YOU

ARTIST IMAGES

BY L©THAR TRAMPERT

Bibliographic information of the German National Library: The German National Library lists this publication in the German National Bibliography; detailed bibliographic data is available on the Internet at dnb.dnb.de.

The automated analysis of the work in order to obtain information, in particular about patterns, trends and correlations in accordance with §44b UrhG ("text and data mining") is prohibited.

Author: Lothar Trampert
Photos: Lothar Trampert

All photos printed here were taken during press interviews by Lothar Trampert, with the consent of the persons depicted for unrestricted journalistic use.

Publisher: BoD · Books on Demand GmbH, Überseering 33, 22297 Hamburg, bod@bod.de

Printed by: Libri Plureos GmbH, Friedensallee 273, 22763 Hamburg

ISBN: 978-3-7693-5680-9

KLICK! SAID MY GERMAN CAMERA

CAN Y◎U SEE ME?

I've never been a real photographer or photo nerd, but I love taking pictures since my teens. Again and again.

"Dark, blurry, grainy – and why this sad black and white ...?" Everyone paints, sees and remembers things differently, and life is colorful enough as it is. I'm glad I've collected these little low-fi visual samples over the last few decades. Some of them are about sadness, showing people who have gone. But all are about the love of music, of sound, of art.

My longtime job was to talk to musicians, portray them and their work through language, through the printed word. Jazz, Rock and Blues musicians, mostly guitarists or bassists, some singers, pianists, drummers also, one saxophone player and some producers. When I asked them at the end of an interview if I could quickly take a few photos, 19 out of 20 of these people said, "Sure, go ahead!"

Unfortunately, I didn't always have my camera with me, or the situation wasn't right, so that many more impressions from interviews remain only as memories – and there are a lot of them. Memories of sometimes great encounters, usually lasting only 30 to 60 minutes, but occasionally half a studio day or longer. When things got personal and/or the artist's family was sitting in the garden or around the barbecue, my job was done for that day. When interviews were absolutely fascinating or moving and we were racing against the record company's schedule, there was definitely no time for photographing. Or we just forgot about it.

But even missed opportunities can be wonderful memories.

The following more than 200 pages document the opportunities taken. You will meet some great musicians, maybe even some of your idols: Blues legends like Albert Collins, B.B. King, Billy Gibbons of ZZ Top, Brian May of Queen, Carlos Santana, Joanna Connor, Eddie Van Halen, Cream bassist Jack Bruce, Genesis' guitarist Steve Hackett, Jazz icons like Allan Holdsworth, James Blood Ulmer, John Scofield, Mick Goodrick, Pat Martino and George Benson, Jennifer Batten, Hole & Smashing Pumpkins bassist Melissa Auf der Maur, the legendary Cool Jazz saxophonist Lee Konitz, Lemmy Kilmister from Motörhead, Steve Lukather and Michael Landau, Robbie Robertson from The Band, King Crimson's Robert Fripp, Ella Zirina, Uli Jon Roth, Zakk Wylde, Mary Halvorson, Robin Trower, Rory Gallagher, Jeff Beck ...

Blues, Jazz, Rock, Alternative and also some Avantgarde artists – all creative people from the last decades. You find detailed photo credits from page 240 onwards. There are also some lesser-known, young artists among, whose wonderful music is yet to be discovered. Go for it!

Special thanks go to my father Matthias, who always loved making photos, which could take quite a while in the days before the advent of fully automatic digital cameras or even smartphones. But he always celebrated it, standing in front of his occasionally somewhat annoyed family, with some kind of devotion that made me feel that there must be something beautiful about photography.

Later, his sister, my aunt Hedwig (sitting beside him on the picture above), gave me my first camera, which I still have. It was a thrill then!

A big Thank You also goes to my former art teacher Volkhard Stürzbecher, who taught me to "just do it", same to Ilga Tick for the art of "Staubwegstempeln", and to Albrecht Piltz and Gerd Schlüter, who made my first interview photo possible, exactly 34 years ago from this day. You will find it in this book. Finally, many thanks to Doris Dörrie for her inspiring writing about writing in "Leben, Schreiben, Atmen", and to Sylvie Atterer of Sailor Entertainment for organizing the meeting with Saul Hudson, from whom I brought one of my all-time favorite shots. Enjoy – and don't forget to listen to the music!

Lothar Trampert   July 17, 2025

RAY DAVIES / THE KINKS

JIMI HAZEL & RICK SKATORE / 24-7 SPYZ

ANIKA NILLES

JEFF BECK

JENNIFER BATTEN

JOE PERRY
BRAD WHITFORD
TOM HAMILTON

20

STEVEN TYLER / AEROSMITH

ALI NEANDER

ALEX GUNIA
ANDY SUMMERS
ALEX PARCHE

ARMAND SABAL-LECCO

26

CHRISTINA ZURHAUSEN
CLEMENS GOTTWALD
ATHINA KONTOU

AXEL FISCHBACHER
JOHN SCOFIELD

BERNHARD PIETSCH
HARRY OELLERS / AXXIS

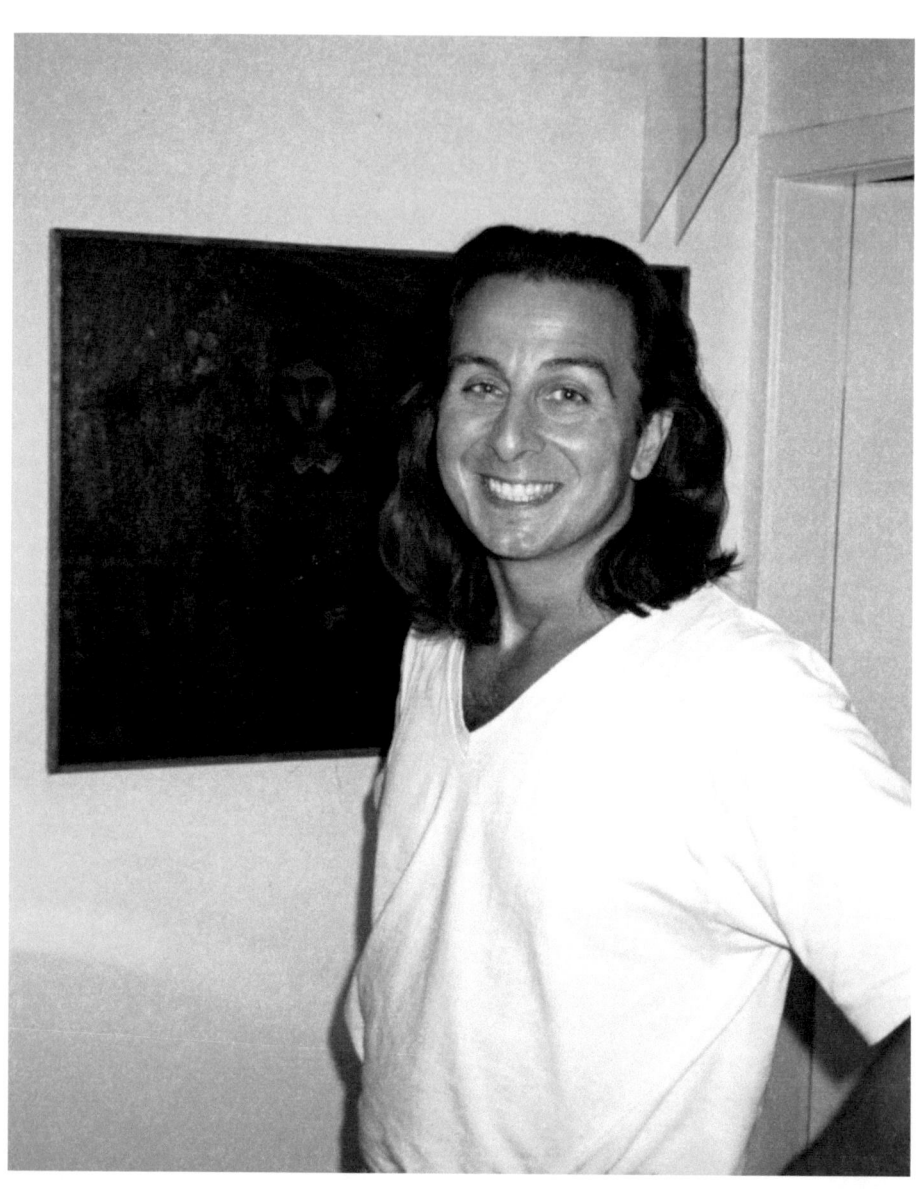

JOEY BALIN
KEITH OLSEN

34

CLARENCE GATEMOUTH BROWN
ALBERT COLLINS

MR. B.B. KING
LUTHER ALLISON
SCREAMIN' JAY HAWKINS

BLUES SARACENO

BRIGITTE HANDLEY

JOSEPH ARTHUR
BRIAN MAY

44

BOB LOG III

LEMMY KILMISTER

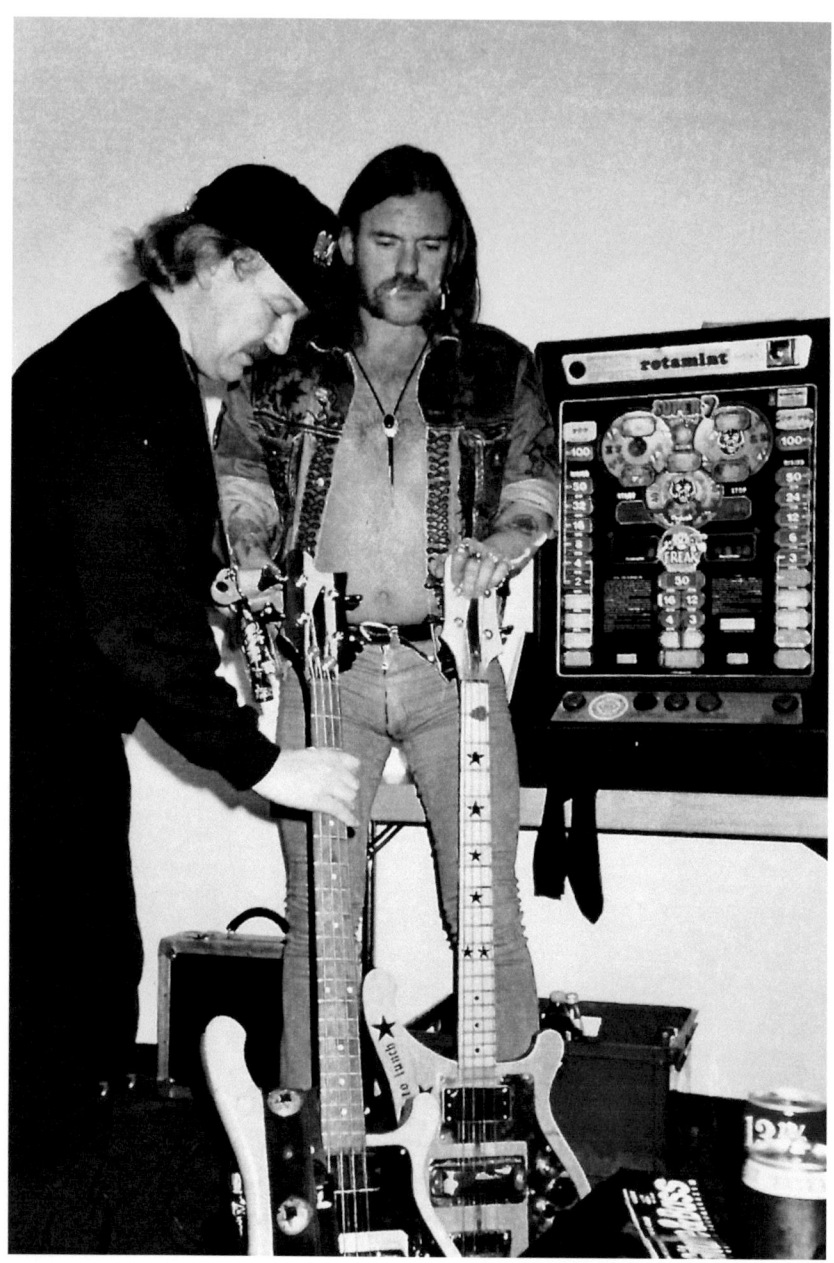

NINA C. ALICE
JOGY RAUTENBERG
JIM VOXX / SKEW SISKIN

JOGY RAUTENBERG
NINA C. ALICE / SKEW SISKIN

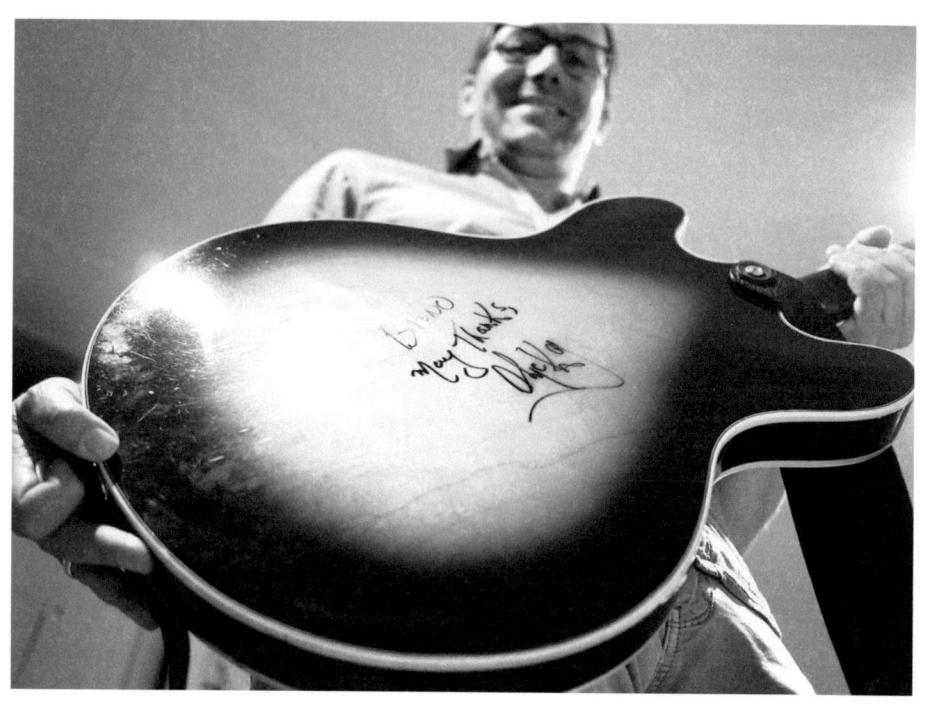

BRUNO MÜLLER

CLAUS FISCHER / FEDERATION OF THE GROOVE

BRUNO MÜLLER
PAUL HELLER

BILLY TEST
HENDRIK SMOCK

MARTIN SASSE
CARIS HERMES
NIKLAS WALTER
STEFAN PFEIFER-GALILEA

MARTIN SASSE

64

PAUL HELLER

TOM PETERSSON
RICK NIELSEN / CHEAP TRICK

CARLOS SANTANA

RAMON KECK / ENDGEGNER
CHRISTINA ZURHAUSEN
JOHANNES STILL
DARIO SCHATTEL

CLEMENS GOTTWALD
SIMON BELOW
CONRAD NOLL
MAREIKE WIENING

CLEM CLEMPSON
MARK CLARKE / COLOSSEUM

DAVE HOLE

GILBY CLARKE
JOIE MASTROKALOS
DUFF MCKAGAN

ALEX VAN HALEN
EDWARD VAN HALEN
ELLA ZIRINA

FRANK WINGOLD

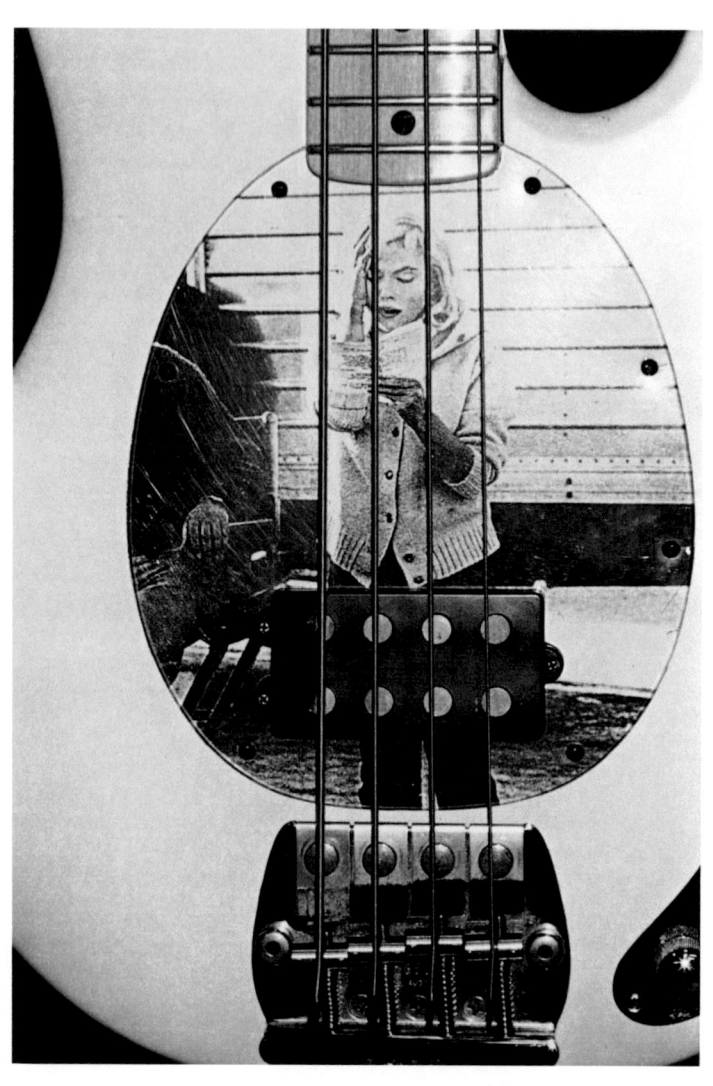

GAIL ANN DORSEY'S BOWIE BASS
CHARLEY STONE
NIGEL HOYLE / GAY DAD

GERALD GRADWOHL

THOMAS KUGI

CHRISTIAN NEANDER

86

GUY PRATT

STEPHAN HINZ
TIM TENAMBERGEN / H-BLOCKX

SHAWN BARTON
ANNE TKACH

90

TONYA LAMM / HAZELDINE

HEITOR PEREIRA / SIMPLY RED
RODRIGO GONZALEZ / DIE ÄRZTE

HUGH CORNWELL / STRANGLERS
MIKE WATT / MINUTEMEN

J MASCIS
& THE FOG
MIKE WATT

JACK BRUCE

JAMES BLOOD ULMER

JAMES BLOOD ULMER
KENNY WAYNE SHEPHERD

CRAIG CALVERT
JAN JAMES

JEFF BUCKLEY

108

JEFF PARKER

JESPER MUNK

AL HENDRIX

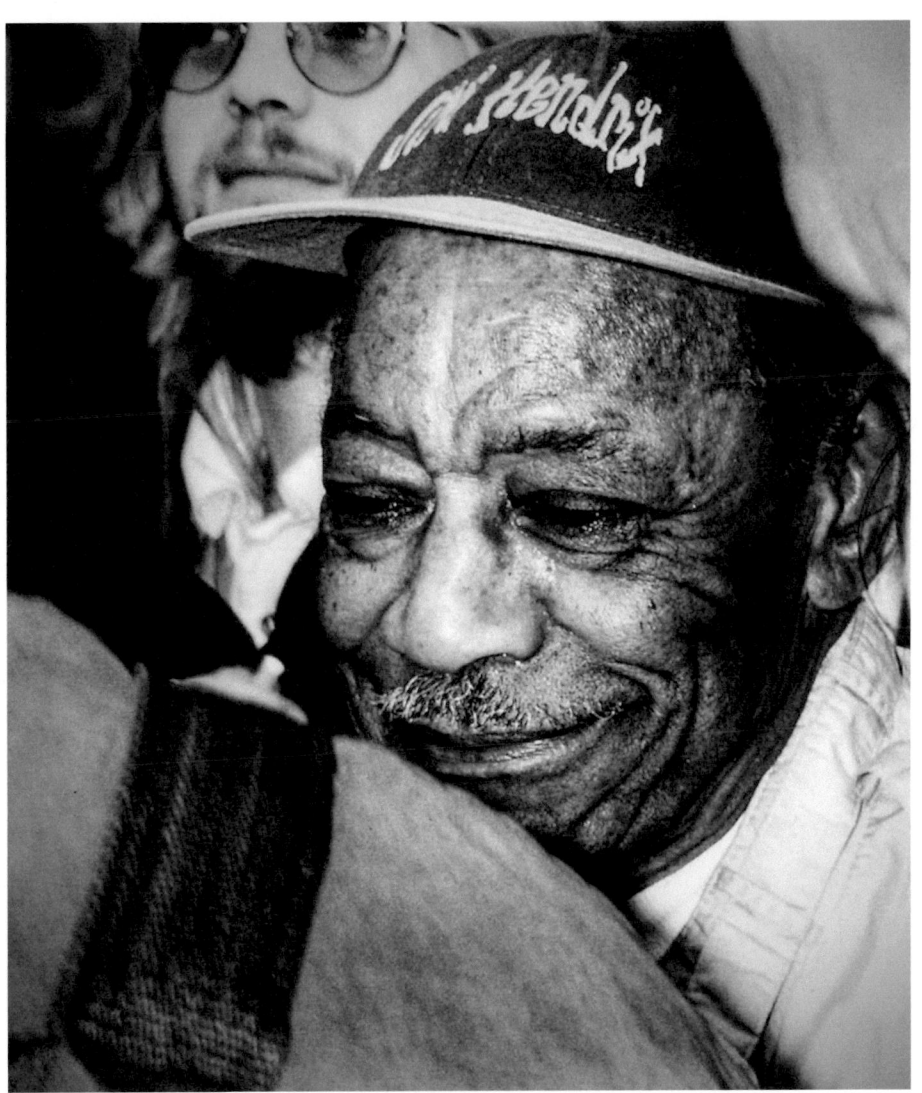

NOEL REDDING
PETE TOWNSHEND

CHRISTIAN VERSPAY
JO JENA

JOE SATRIANI
DEEP PURPLE

JOHN PAUL JONES / LED ZEPPELIN
JOHN HAMMOND JR.

JOHN PETRUCCI / DREAM THEATER
JOHN SHANKS

MARTIN SIMON
GÖTZ WIDMANN / JOINT VENTURE
JOHN SNYDER

KEB MO
KEZIAH JONES

KIM SALMON & THE SURREALISTS

LEE KONITZ

134

LUISE VOLKMANN
& LEONESAUVAGE

THE INCREDIBLE MR. SMITH

MARTIN SCHMIDT / THE RAZORBLADES

LAGE LUND

MARY HALVORSON
SYLVIE COURVOISIER

MAX PROSA
NAIMA HUSSEINI

MELISSA AUF DER MAUR / HOLE

144

MICHAEL KAROLI / CAN

146

ULI JON ROTH
MICHAEL KATON

MICHAEL LANDAU

150

MICHAEL SCHENKER

MICK GOODRICK

KAT KRAFT
MIKE KENEALLY

TEDDY LANDAU
MICHAEL LANDAU / THE RAGING HONKIES

TONY KANAL
TOM DUMONT / NO DOUBT

STEVE LUKATHER / TOTO

MIKE PORCARO / TOTO

MIKE STERN

NGUYEN LE
PAT MARTINO

GEORGE BENSON
WERNER NEUMANN

168

PENNYWISE
PORNOMAT

ZAKK WYLDE

JAMES LOMENZO
ZAKK WYLDE / PRIDE & GLORY

KIP WINGER
REB BEACH

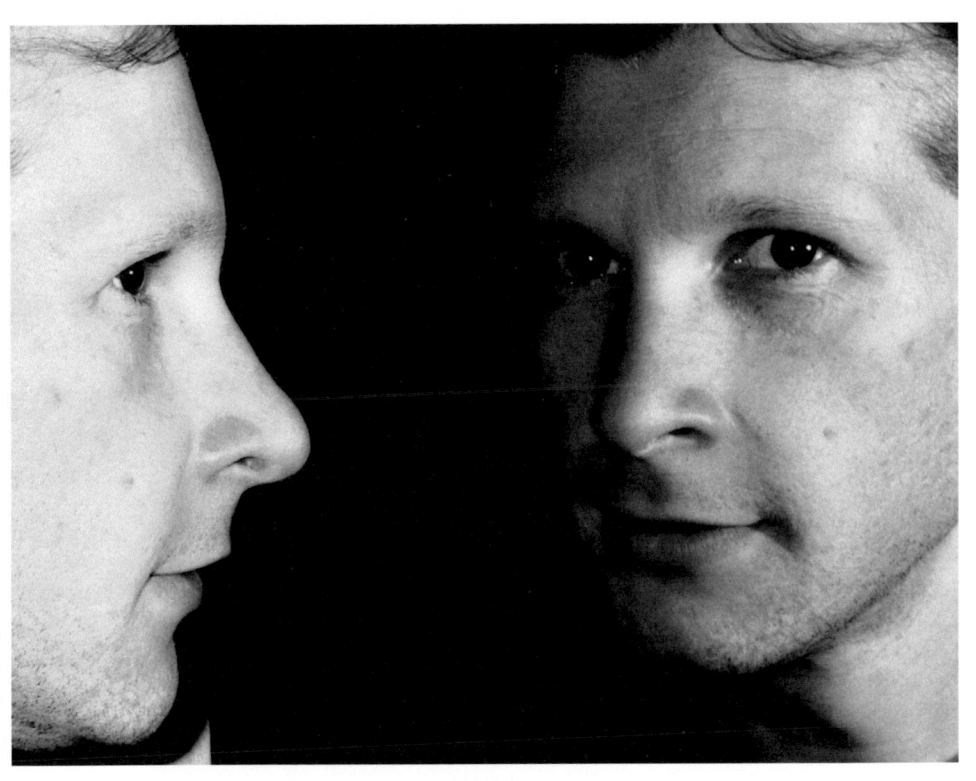

RON SPIELMAN
RON SPIEGELMAN

ROB THOMAS
ROBIN TROWER

ROBBIE ROBERTSON / THE BAND

CHRIS CORNER / SNEAKER PIMPS

ROBERT FRIPP / KING CRIMSON

RORY GALLAGHER

WALTER WOLFMAN WASHINGTON
JOANNA CONNOR

SARA K.

SEBASTIAN GRAMSS / METEORS

STEFAN STOPPOK

STEVE BAILEY

STEPHAN BRINGS

STEVE HACKETT
JOHN HACKETT

MATHIS RICHTER-REICHHELM
A. JAY HALE / SWIMMING THE NILE

MATHIS RICHTER-REICHHELM

200

SNAIL'S PACE SLIM / THE HAMSTERS

TOBIAS HOFFMANN

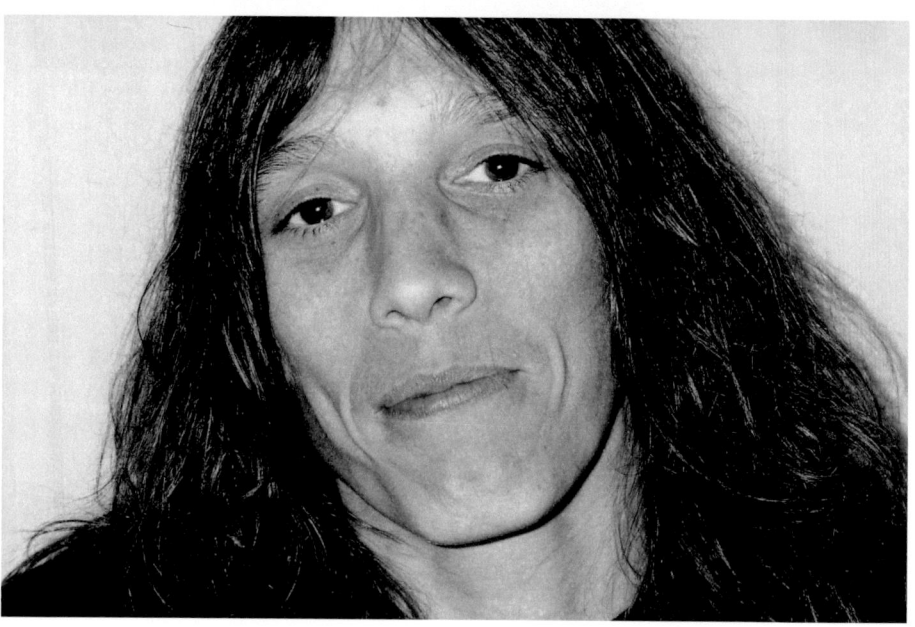

TOM PETTY
TONY LEVIN
BRIAN KEITH / TESLA

TOM SCHWOLL
FLEUR DE MALHEUR

TROY NEWMAN

VERNON REID / LIVING COLOUR
NORWOOD FISHER / FISHBONE

TORI AMOS
WILLY PORTER

WARREN CUCCURULLO / DURAN DURAN

WOLFGANG MUTHSPIEL

DIETER ILG

GARY ROSSINGTON
RANDALL HALL / LYNYRD SKYNYRD

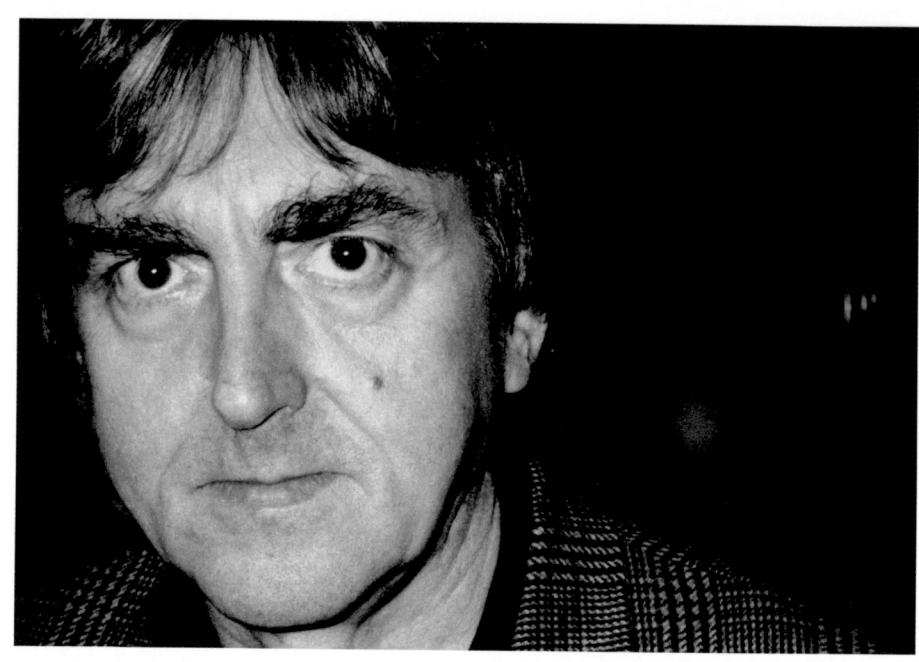

ALLAN HOLDSWORTH

STEVIE SALAS

MICHELLE MELDRUM / PHANTOM BLUE

ROGER GLOVER / DEEP PURPLE

CHRIS WHITLEY

CHRIS WHITLEY

ALI CLAUDI

230

ALI CLAUDI

HARDY FISCHOETTER

MICHAEL SAGMEISTER
PAT MARTINO

BILLY GIBBONS
DUSTY HILL / ZZ TOP

FAN MAN
SAUL HUDSON

SLASH / GUNS N' ROSES

PH⊙TO FACTS

20
JOE PERRY
BRAD WHITFORD
TOM HAMILTON
STEVEN TYLER / AEROSMITH
23.11.1993
Westfalenhalle
Dortmund, Germany
23.06.1994
Seidenstickerhalle
Bielefeld, Germany

22
ALI NEANDER / RODGAU MONOTONES
09.02.2000 Frankfurt Music Fair
Frankfurt, Germany

24
ALEX GUNIA
15.08.2020
Rhenania
Köln, Germany

ANDY SUMMERS / THE POLICE
04.12.1995
Live Club
Rome, Italy

ALEX PARCHE / ZELTINGER
01.02.1993
Home
Köln, Germany

26
ARMAND SABAL-LECCO
08.03.1994
Home
West Hollywood LA, USA

28
CHRISTINA ZURHAUSEN
CLEMENS GOTTWALD
ATHINA KONTOU
12/2022
Artheater
Köln, Germany

30
AXEL FISCHBACHER
09.03.2017
My Office
Köln, Germany

JOHN SCOFIELD
14.01.2002
Steigenberger Frankfurter Hof
Frankfurt, Germany

32
BERNHARD PIETSCH
HARRY OELLERS / AXXIS
28.11.1994
Goodnight L.A. Studio
Los Angeles, USA

34
JOEY BALIN / PRODUCER
23.02.1994
Home
Köln-Deutz, Germany

KEITH OLSEN / PRODUCER
28.11.1994
Goodnight L.A. Studio
Los Angeles, USA

36
CLARENCE GATEMOUTH BROWN
14.02.1995
Cafe Central
Köln, Germany

ALBERT COLLINS
18.07.1993
Tanzbrunnen
Köln, Germany

38
B.B. KING
12.11.1992
Alte Oper
Frankfurt, Germany

LUTHER ALLISON
18.11.1992
Cafe @ Hauptbahnhof
Köln, Germany

40
BLUES SARACENO / POISON
05.05.1995
N. Highland Avenue
Hollywood L.A., USA

42
BRIGITTE HANDLEY
22.04.2017
Silvertone Recordstore
Köln, Germany

44
JOSEPH ARTHUR
17.04.2000
Stadtgarten
Köln, Germany

BRIAN MAY / QUEEN
18.12.1992
Möwenpick Hotel
Bielefeld, Germany

46
BOB LOG III
15.12.1998
Underground
Köln, Germany

48
LEMMY KILMISTER / MOTÖRHEAD
20.12.1992
Philipshalle
Düsseldorf, Germany

52
JIM VOXX
JOGI RAUTENKRANZ
NINA C. ALICE / SKEW SISKIN
05.07.1997
Home / Club
Berlin, Germany

56
BRUNO MÜLLER
05/2022
Home
Köln-Rondorf, Germany

58
CLAUS FISCHER
BRUNO MÜLLER
PAUL HELLER
08.09.2022
Stadtgarten
Köln, Germany

60
BILLY TEST
12.09.2022
Urania Theater
Köln, Germany

HENDRIK SMOCK
08.09.2022
Stadtgarten
Köln, Germany

62
MARTIN SASSE
CARIS HERMES
NIKLAS WALTER
STEFAN PFEIFER-GALILEA
12.09.2022
Urania Theater
Köln, Germany

64
MARTIN SASSE
PAUL HELLER
12.09.2022
Urania Theater
Köln, Germany

66
TOM PETERSSON
RICK NIELSEN / CHEAP TRICK
16.03.1994
Hyatt Regency Cologne
Köln, Germany

CARLOS SANTANA
My very first interview.
17.07.1991
Tanzbrunnen Open Air
Köln, Germany

68
CHRISTINA ZURHAUSEN
JOHANNES STILL
DARIO SCHATTEL
RAMON KECK / ENDGEGNER
21.11.2023
Lost Level Club
Köln, Germany

70
CLEMENS GOTTWALD
SIMON BELOW
CONRAD NOLL
MAREIKE WIENING
08.11.2023
Fiffi Bar
Köln, Germany

72
CLEM CLEMPSON
MARK CLARKE / COLOSSEUM
27.10.1994
E-Werk
Köln, Germany

74
DAVE HOLE
13.01.1994
Essen, Germany

76
GILBY CLARKE / GUNS N' ROSES
13.09.1994 or 08.07.1997
Virgin Records
Köln, Germany

JOIE MASTROKALOS
DUFF MCKAGAN / GUNS N' ROSES
18.10.1993
Hotel Westfalenpark
Dortmund, Germany

78
ALEX VAN HALEN
EDWARD VAN HALEN
22.11.1994
Home / 5150 Studio
Hollywood L.A., USA

ELLA ZIRINA
02.04.2023
Klaeng Festival Stadtgarten
Köln, Germany

80
FRANK WINGOLD
16.04.2021
Home
Köln, Germany

82
GAIL ANN DORSEY'S BASS / DAVID BOWIE
30.01.1996 or 13.06.1997
Westfalenhalle
Dortmund, Germany

CHARLEY STONE
NIGEL HOYLE / GAY DAD
22.06.1999
Warner Music Office
Hamburg, Germany

84
GERALD GRADWOHL
THOMAS KUGI
10/2023
Topos
Leverkusen, Germany

86
CHRISTIAN NEANDER / SELIG & KUNGFU
07.07.1999
BMG RecordS Office
Köln, Germany

GUY PRATT / PINK FLOYD
11.03.1995
Musikmesse
Frankfurt, Germany

88
STEPHAN HINZ
TIM TENAMBERGEN / H-BLOCKX
21.08.1994
Hotel am Ring
Köln, Germany
05.03.1996
Home / Studio
Münster, Germany

90
SHAWN BARTON
ANNE TKACH
TONYA LAMM / HAZELDINE
26.11.1998
Kantine
Köln, Germany

92
HEITOR PEREIRA / SIMPLY RED
16.02.1994
Club Gig
Hamburg, Germany
or
01.02.1994
Hotel Room
London, UK

RODRIGO GONZALEZ / DIE ÄRZTE
19.08.1994
Popkomm
Köln, Germany

94
HUGH CORNWELL / STRANGLERS
02.07.1997
Hotel Crystall
Köln, Germany

MIKE WATT / MINUTEMEN
04.12.2000
Luxor
Köln, Germany

96
J MASCIS & THE FOG
MIKE WATT
04.12.2000
Luxor
Köln, Germany

98
JACK BRUCE / CREAM
04.11.1992
CMP Studio
Zerkall, Germany

100
JAMES BLOOD ULMER
24.10.1991
Club
Essen, Germany

102
KENNY WAYNE SHEPHERD
03.07.1998
Record Company Office
Hamburg, Germany

104
CRAIG CALVERT
JAN JAMES
07.12.1994
Hotel
Köln, Germany

106
JEFF BUCKLEY
08.07.1995
Kleines E-Werk
Köln, Germany

108
JEFF PARKER / TORTOISE
07.11.2022
Urania Theater
Köln, Germany

110
JESPER MUNK
13.11.2024
Jaki Club Stadtgarten,
Köln, Germany

112
AL HENDRIX / FATHER OF JIMI
14.09.1997
Händel House
London, UK

114
NOEL REDDING / JIMI HENDRIX EXPERIENCE
PETE TOWNSHEND
14.09.1997
Händel House
London, UK

116
CHRISTIAN VERSPAY
JO JENA
03.04.2023
Loft
Köln, Germany

118
JOE SATRIANI
01.03.1993
Hotel Rudolfplatz
Köln, Germany
04.02.1998
Hotel Crystall
Köln, Germany

DEEP PURPLE
07.06.1994
Westfalenhalle
Dortmund, Germany

120
JOHN PAUL JONES / LED ZEPPELIN
15.07.1999
Chelsea Hotel
Köln, Germany

JOHN HAMMOND JR.
20.10.1992
Forum
Leverkusen, Germany

122
JOHN PETRUCCI / DREAM THEATER
05.11.1993
Biskuithalle
Bonn, Germany

JOHN SHANKS / PRODUCER
on tour with Melissa Etheridge
05.02.1996
Sporthalle
Köln, Germany

124
JOINT VENTURE
Götz Widmann
Martin Simon
16.08.1999
My home
Köln, Germany

JOHN SNYDER / PRODUCER
14.02.1995
Cafe Central
Köln, Germany

126
KEB MO
27.07.1996 or 13.07.1998
Hotel
Köln, Germany

KEZIAH JONES
05.11.1992
Virgin Records Office
Köln, Germany

130
KIM SALMON & THE SURREALISTS
28.01.1994
Underground Club
Köln, Germany

132
LEE KONITZ
04.12.2016
Altes Pfandhaus
Köln, Germany

136
LUISE VOLKMANN & LEONESAUVAGE
19.12.2022
Niehler Freiheit
Köln, Germany

138
MARTIN SCHMIDT / THE RAZORBLADES
28.10.2022
Kult 41
Bonn, Germany

140
LAGE LUND
24.05.2023
Jaki / Stadtgarten
Köln, Germany

MARY HALVORSON
SYLVIE COURVOISIER
10.10.2018
Stadtgarten
Köln, Germany

142
MAX PROSA
25.09.2022
Helios 37
Köln, Germany

NAIMA HUSSEINI
28.10.2016
Die Wohngemeinschaft
Köln, Germany

144
MELISSA AUF DER MAUR / HOLE
21.04.1995
Live Music Hall
Köln, Germany

146
MICHAEL KAROLI / CAN
26.03.1999
Cafe Central
Köln, Germany

148
ULI JON ROTH / ELECTRIC SUN
27.05.1998
Stahlwerk
Düsseldorf, Germany

MICHAEL KATON
04/1993
Cafe Ehrenstraße
Köln, Germany

150
MICHAEL LANDAU / SESSION PLAYER
08.03.1994
Home / Pacific Palisades
Los Angeles, USA

152
MICHAEL SCHENKER / MSG & UFO
02.10.1997
Hotel Friesenplatz
Köln, Germany

154
MICK GOODRICK
08.03.1995
CMP Studio
Zerkall, Germany

156
KAT KRAFT / VIXEN
Kat was a journalist colleague and
also drummer with the band Vixen.
04.05.1995
Capitol Records Studios
Hollywood, Los Angeles USA

MIKE KENEALLY / FRANK ZAPPA BAND
06.05.1995
Cafe M.I.T.
Hollywood, Los Angeles USA

158
TEDDY LANDAU
MICHAEL LANDAU / THE RAGING HONKIES
08.05.95
Pacific Palisades
Los Angeles, USA

TONY KANAL
TOM DUMONT / NO DOUBT
17.03.1997
Live Music Hall
Köln, Germany

160
STEVE LUKATHER / TOTO
03/1994
Home
Hollywood Hills, Los Angeles USA

162
MIKE PORCARO / TOTO
23.11.1994
Home
North Hollywood Valley, Los Angeles USA
04.05.1995
Capitol Records Studios
Hollywood, Los Angeles USA

164
MIKE STERN
03.11.1991
FZ Garath
Düsseldorf, Germany

166
NGUYEN LE
24.01.1995
Senats Hotel
Köln, Germany

PAT MARTINO
14.09.2000
Ideal Tonstudio
Osnabrück, Germany

168
GEORGE BENSON
07.07.1993
Warner Records
Hamburg, Germany

WERNER NEUMANN / DREI VOM RHEIN
19.08.1999
Home
Köln-Weiss, Germany

170
FLETCHER DRAGGE
RANDY BRADBURY / PENNYWISE
07.05.1999
Hotel Crystall
Köln, Germany

SASCHA STADLER
REINER KALLAS
SIEBETH / PORNOMAT
11.08.1998
Polydor Label Boat Party
Hamburg, Germany

172
ZAKK WYLDE / PRIDE & GLORY
Support of ZZ Top
08.07.1994
Westfalenhalle
Dortmund, Germany

174
JAMES LOMENZO / PRIDE & GLORY
08.07.1994
Westfalenhalle
Dortmund, Germany

176
KIP WINGER
REB BEACH / WINGER
04.05.1993
Maritim Hotel
Köln, Germany

RON SPIELMAN
05.03.1996
Batschkapp
Frankfurt, German

178
ROB THOMAS / MATCHBOX TWENTY
18.04.2000
Hyatt Regency Cologne
Köln, Germany

ROBIN TROWER
26.11.1994
House Of Blues
Hollywood, Los Angeles USA

180
ROBBIE ROBERTSON / THE BAND
25.10.1994
Hyatt Regency
Köln, Germany

182
CHRIS CORNER / SNEAKER PIMPS
26.08.1999
Virgin Records Office
Köln, Germany

ROBERT FRIPP / KING CRIMSON
18.09.1998
Home
Salisbury, UK

184
RORY GALLAGHER
14.12.1992
Hotel
Bonn, Germany

186
WALTER WOLFMAN WASHINGTON
19.04.1995
Hyatt Regency Cologne
Köln, Germany

JOANNA CONNOR
26.04.1994
Cafe Aachener Straße
Köln, Germany

188
SARA K.
06.05.1996
Zakk
Düsseldorf, Germany

190
SEBASTIAN GRAMSS / METEORS
01.09.2024
Stadtgarten
Köln, Germany

192
STEFAN STOPPOK
14.01.1997
Home / Studio
Essen, Germany

194
STEVE BAILEY
08.05.1995
N. Highland Avenue
Hollywood L.A., USA

STEPHAN BRINGS / BRINGS
09.04.1992
Underground Club
Köln, Germany

196
STEVE HACKETT
JOHN HACKETT
04/2000
Home / Atelier
London, UK

198
MATHIS RICHTER-REICHHELM
A. JAY HALE / SWIMMING THE NILE
03.02.1993
Live Club
Hamburg, Germany

200
SNAIL'S PACE SLIM / THE HAMSTERS
07.11.1995
Herbrand's Club
Köln, Germany

202
TOBIAS HOFFMANN
08/2022
Home
Köln, Germany

204
TOM PETTY
14.09.1994
Hotel Atlantik
Hamburg, Germany

BRIAN KEITH / TESLA
21.07.1994
WOM or Virgin Records
Köln, Germany

TONY LEVIN
on tour with the Peter Gabriel Band
10.11.1993
Westfalenhalle
Dortmund, Germany
or
01.03.1996
Virgin Records
Köln, Germany

206
TOM SCHWOLL / JINGO DE LUNCH
FLEUR DE MALHEUR
16.02.2024
33 1/3 Record Store
Duisburg, Germmany

208
TROY NEWMAN
09.02.1995
Hotel Bar
Hamburg, Germany

210
VERNON REID / LIVING COLOUR
06/1996
Stadtgarten
Köln, Germany

NORWOOD FISHER / FISHBONE
01.02.2000
Hyatt Regency Cologne
Köln, Germany

212
TORI AMOS
10.07.1995
Countryside
Dublin, Ireland

WILLY PORTER
16.12.1995
Record Company Showcase
Köln, Germany

214
WARREN CUCCURULLO / DURAN DURAN
05/2000
Hotel Wasserturm
Köln, Germany

216
WOLFGANG MUTHSPIEL
06.05.1998
Loft
Köln, Germany

218
DIETER ILG
06.05.1998
Loft
Köln, Germany

220
GARY ROSSINGTON
RANDALL HALL / LYNYRD SKYNYRD
17.12.1991
Studio / Practise Room
St. Augustine, USA

222
STEVIE SALAS / SASS JORDAN BAND
on tour opening for Aerosmith
23.06.1994
Seidenstickerhalle
Bielefeld, Germany

ALLAN HOLDSWORTH
19.03.1997
Bayrischer Hof
München, Germany
or
10.03.1994
Home / Studio
Vista CA, USA

224
MICHELLE MELDRUM / PHANTOM BLUE
21.10.1993
Roadrunner Records Office
Köln, Germany

ROGER GLOVER / DEEP PURPLE
Deep Purple
07.06.1994
Westfalenhalle
Dortmund, Germany

226
CHRIS WHITLEY
10.10.2003
MTC Club
Köln, Germany

230
ALI CLAUDI
14.09.2022
Streckstrump
Köln, Germany

234
HARDY FISCHÖTTER
14.09.2022
Em Streckstrump
Köln, Germany

236
MICHAEL SAGMEISTER
PAT MARTINO
14.09.2000
Ideal Tonstudio
Osnabrück, Germany

BILLY GIBBONS
DUSTY HILL / ZZ TOP
09.04.1994
Warner Records Office
Köln, Germany

238
FAN MAN
SAUL HUDSON
SLASH / GUNS N' ROSES
07.04.2024
Hyatt Regency Cologne
Köln, Germany

THE AUTHOR

Lothar Trampert loves Jazz, Rock, Funk, Classical music, Blues, R&B, as well as electric guitars, good weather, cycling, cats and photography.

He studied musicology and art history. Since 1990 he worked as a freelance journalist and author, was then music editor of a musician's magazine for more than 30 years, has conducted about 400 interviews with artists of all genres and written about almost as many old guitars and basses.

Under the pseudonym Jan Urbanek, he released the autofictional novel "Popsog" (2024). In May 2025 he published "Jimi Hendrix. Musician Popstar Icon", an almanach about the man, the musician, his instruments, inspirations and influences. More about that on www.jimihendrixbuch.de

His new book "See You" is a trip through the past decades. And about memories.

CONTACT ME

Follow my blog on www.paleblueice.com
Mail: lothar.trampert@netcologne.de

I welcome criticism, corrections, opinions & invitations to coffee.
Even tea. Worldwide.

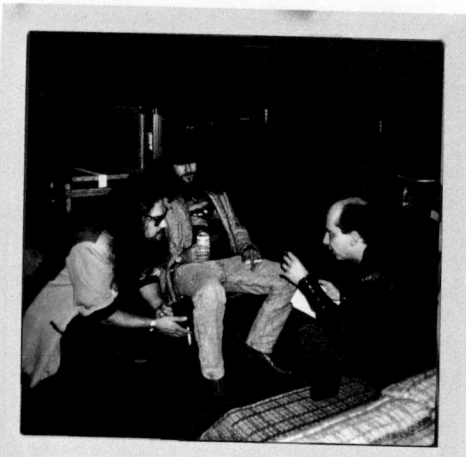

THANK Y◎U

Al Hendrix
Albert Collins
Albrecht Piltz
Alex Gunia
Alex Parche
Alex Van Halen
Ali Neander
Allan Holdsworth
Andy Summers
Anika Nilles
Anne Tkach
Armand Sabal-Lecco
Athina Kontou
Axel Fischbacher
B.B. King
Billy Gibbons
Billy Test
Blues Saraceno
Bob Log III
Brad Whitford
Brian Henry Hooper
Brian May
Brian Wheat
Brigitte Handley
Bruno Müller
Caris Hermes
Carlos Santana
Charley Stone
Chris Corner
Chris Whitley
Christian Lorenzen
Christian Neander
Christian Verspay
Christina Zurhausen
Clarence Gatemouth Brown
Claus Fischer

Clem Clempson
Clemens Gottwald
Conrad Noll
Dave Hole
Dieter Ilg
Dominik Mahnig
Doris Dörrie
Duff McKagan
Dusty Hill
Ed King
Eddie Van Halen
Ella Zirina
Fletcher Dragge
Frank Wingold
Gail Ann Dorsey
Gary Rossington
George Benson
Gerald Gradwohl
Gerd Schlüter
Gilby Clarke
Götz Widmann
Greg Calvert
Guy Pratt
Hedwig Hauer
Heitor
Hendrik Smock
Hildegard Schmidt
Hugh Cornwell
Ilga Tick
J. Mascis
Jack Bruce
James Blood Ulmer
James LoMenzo
Jan James
jan Urbanek
Jay Hale

Jeff Beck
Jeff Buckley
Jeff Keith
Jeff Parker
Jennifer Batten
Jim Voxx
Jimii Hazel
Jo Jena
Joanna Connor
Joe Perry
Joe Satriani
Joey Balin
Jogy Rautenberg
John Hackett
John Hammond
John Paul Jones
John Petrucci
John Scofield
John Shanks
John Snyder
Joie Mastrokalos
Jonas Engel
Joseph Arthur
Kat Kraft
Keb Mo
Keith Olsen
Kenny Wayne Shepherd
Keziah Jones
Kim Salmon
Kip Winger
Lage Lund
Lee Konitz
Lemmy Kilmister
Leonhard Huhn
Luise Volkmann
Luther Allison

Mareike Wiening
Margo Dee
Marion Kraft
Mark Clarke
Martin Kleinti Simon
Martin Sasse
Martin Schmidt
Mary Halvorson
Mathis Richter-Reichhelm
Matthias Trampert
Max Prosa
Melissa Auf Der Maur
Michael Karoli
Michael Katon
Michael Landau
Michael Sagmeister
Michael Schenker
Michelle Meldrum
Mick Goodrick
Mike Keneally
Mike Porcaro
Mike Stern
Mike Watt
Naima Husseini
Nguyen Le
Nigel Hoyle
Nina C. Alice
Noel Redding
Norwood Fisher
Pat Martino
Paul Heller
Phil Campbell
Philip Zoubek
Ramon Keck
Randall Hall
Randy Bradbury

Ray Davies
Reb Beach
Rick Nielsen
Rick Skatore
Rob Thomas
Robbie Robertson
Robert Fripp
Robin Trower
Rodrigo Gonzalez
Roger Glover
Ron Spielman
Rory Gallagher
Sara K
Sascha Stadler
Sebastian Gramss
Shannon Barnett
Shawn Barton
Siebeth Sonne
Simon Below
Slash
Snail's Pace Slim
Stefan Stoppok
Stephan Brings
Stephan Hinz
Steve Bailey
Steve Hackett
Steve Lukather
Steven Tyler
Stevie Salas
Sylvie Atterer
Sylvie Courvoisier
Teddy Landau
Tim Humpe
Tobias Hoffmann
Tom Dumont
Tom Hamilton

Tom Peterson
Tom Petty
Tom Schwoll
Tony Kanal
Tony Levin
Tonya Lamm
Tori Amos
Troy Newman
Uli Jon Roth
Vernon Reid
Volkhard Stürzbecher
Walter Pietsch
Walter Wolfman Washington
Warren Cuccurullo
Werner Neumann
Willy Porter
Wolfgang Muthspiel
Zakk Wylde ©